Human Resource Management

Employees and Employers in Action

Cynthia Fontelle and Louis Bevoc

Published by
NutriNiche System LLC

Louis Bevoc books...simple explanations of complex subjects

Introduction

In terms of organizations, human resources are the people who make up the workforce. Often used interchangeably with "human capital," human resources drive growth and prosperity. Without these resources, organizations would cease to exist.

Human resource departments exist with organizations to oversee many aspects of employment including hiring, retaining, promoting, training, disciplining, and firing employees. Personnel in these departments understand the legal aspects of management actions and employee behavior, and they work to maintain positive management/employee relationships.

Human resource management (HRM) is all about the management of people and workplace cultures. It uses strategies designed to meet management objectives by maximizing employee performance. These strategies incorporate the goals of organizational leaders while adhering to government laws, rules established by collective bargaining agreements, and other regulatory requirements.

Before launching into the description and exemplification of human resource management, it is important to understand a little bit about the history of the subject matter. Human resource departments were created in the early 20th century to handle the management/labor disputes that often led to costly employee strikes. The thinking at the time was that these departments would listen to worker grievances and offer solutions to resolve them before they festered into much larger issues that could potentially shut down companies temporarily or, in worst-case scenarios, permanently.

Fast forward to the late 20th century (more specifically the 1970s), and the business world faced major challenges from deregulation, technological advances, and, most importantly, the influx of global competition. These challenges forced companies to hire people and find better ways to utilize existing employees; thereby creating a new set of problems. HRM offered solutions to these problems by formulating strategies that focused on people rather than the tasks they needed to accomplish to achieve organizational objectives.

The HRM strategies from the 1970s worked, but they achieved goals using different methodologies. One method was micro-management driven while the other had a macro-management focus. These two methods are described below for a better understanding of each.

Micro-management

This HRM method employed a hands-on approach where people were managed using structured processes and procedures. In other words, rules were put in place that dictated how people behaved in the workplace. Good behavior was encouraged using rewards such as paid time off or monetary compensation and bad behavior was discouraged with punishments such as reprimands, demotions, or suspensions.

Micromanagement is often associated with negativity due to the required strict adherence to established protocol. Employees must conform or they are put on a program for improvement. If they cannot improve then they risk demotion or termination. This negative association bears some truth, but it is not always the case. In some instances, micro-management HRM is beneficial. For example, it works very well in military combat situations where deviance from rules could result in people being killed.

Macro-management

This method of HRM uses a hands-off approach. It gets away from strict adherence to rules and regulations and focuses more on management/employee harmony. People find happiness at work by being involved in decision making processes and knowing that their employer truly cares about their well-being.

Macro-management is thought of as good by many people. This thinking is warranted because people feel like they are an active part of the company, helping to guide it towards success. However, the downside to this methodology is some people stop producing when they are not being showered with attention. They end up having no self-motivation which has a big impact on their productivity and, consequently, the success of the organizations that employ them.

Today's HRM methodology is a combination of micro-management and macro-management. Rules and regulations are in place to maintain order, but there is also a focus on the human element so employees can find happiness and satisfaction at work. When operating as planned, this mixture works quite well for workers and management. However, as most people are aware, everything does not always go as planned so companies can experience "bumps in the road."

Interestingly, the rules and regulations of HRM today might be more stringent then they have ever been in the past. This might appear to oppose management/employee harmony, but it is actually justified and understandable based on the changes that workplaces have experienced. Increases in issues such as sexual harassment and workplace violence have forced organizations to become more specific and stern in terms of how they expect employees to behave. Written policies and procedures protect employees from harm and prevent organizations from facing lawsuits that can be lengthy and expensive. However, companies need to be careful here because too many rules can result in people disliking their place of work...so they look for employment elsewhere.

The human element of HRM takes into account the famous Hawthorne Studies conducted in the 1920s where it was discovered employees' motivation stems from the attention being paid to them rather than the conditions they work under. Researchers Elton Mayo and Fritz Roethlisberger found that, assuming conditions are not terrible (temperature, ergonomics, stress, fatigue, etc.), workers will increase their output when rewards are provided, and those rewards include management taking an interest in their jobs. The only problem with this philosophy is that those same workers will decrease their output once management loses interest in their jobs. In other words, their motivation will not permanently increase.

Now you understand a little about the history of HRM, so let's move forward to the crux of this book that illustrates how HRM functions in workplaces.

In action

This section is informative, interesting, educational, and, in some cases, entertaining. It shows how HRM works and why it is needed in organizations. It also provides and explains the benefits of human resource professionals along with the challenges that they face. Finally, it provides a foundation for those seeking basic knowledge, and it leaves the reader with greater appreciations for the subject matter.

Let's start by discussing HRM and its involvement with leadership.

Leadership

Ultimately, the goals of the human resource departments reflect the goals of leadership, and HRM is a strategy designed to achieve those goals. This strategy involves motivating employees so they become more productive when doing their jobs. As productivity improves, so does the bottom line...which is typically a major goal of leaders. In short, HRM strategies help employees become motivated to follow the paths that their leaders have chosen.

HRM also helps leaders spot employees who are capable of moving into management positions. Strategic thinking is used to find workers who are capable of advancement and developing them so they can take on new roles. This development process is critical because, without it, some employees do not have the necessary understanding and skills to advance...so they end up failing. This failure impacts the employees and their organizations; thereby creating lose/lose situations.

Another aspect of HRM strategy involves change. More specifically, it helps employees accept the changes made by organizational leaders. Change can be very difficult without some type of mitigation procedure in place, and HRM provides that procedure.

Sometimes change acceptance comes with education designed to reduce fear of the unknown while other times it comes with rewards offered as incentives. However, regardless of the method used, human resource professionals typically have the experience necessary for driving the overall change management strategy.

The key to the success of HRM and leadership is collaboration. Human resource personnel need to work together with leaders to develop employees and get them to buy into the culture and direction of the organization. This development begins at the time of hiring and takes place throughout employee lifecycles. Training, which will be discussed in more detail later, is critical for the developmental process because it provides the skills necessary for people and organizations to grow and prosper.

Below is an example of the collaboration of HRM and leadership at a Lamar Transport, an automotive corporation that owns five car dealerships.

Lamar Transport

Leadership at Lamar Transport has made the selling of electric cars a top priority because research has shown that they are the future of the automobile industry. The CEO, Stan Watson, meets with the Human Resources Manager, Marjorie Newport, to discuss a plan of action to get employees at the company to buy into the change.

At the meeting, Stan and Marjorie conclude that the only employees at Lamar who will resist this change are the salespeople. Office and staff personnel will support the change because the engine power source has little bearing on their jobs. Since all of the dealerships have eliminated their service centers, there are no mechanics who will struggle with obtaining the skills necessary to work on electric cars. This leaves the salespeople, and they might present a major challenge. Their acceptance of the change is critical because they are the most visible employees at Lamar, and they play the biggest role in getting the cars to the customers. If they get on board with the electric concept and move vehicles, then other employees will ride the wave of success and be inspired to perform to the best of their abilities.

To combat the potential change acceptance issue, Marjorie develops a two-part HRM strategy that targets the salespeople. Part one involves training that will highlight the benefits of electric cars from an environmental, cost-saving, and noise perspective. The focus of the training will be on the following:

- Electric vehicles are good for the environment because they reduce the burning of fossil fuels that pollute the air. Pollution reduction is something that certain people believe in strongly, and they spend their money to support those beliefs by purchasing electric cars.
- Some people are not interested in environmental concerns, but they are interested in saving money...and gas costs money that is not needed for electric vehicles.
- Noise is something that most people dislike, and electric cars generate far less more noise than gas-burning vehicles.

Regardless of the reason, electric cars have advantages that can be used to sell them. Training will educate the salespeople so they are better prepared to answer questions and provide the information necessary to entice buyers and close sales.

Part two of the HRM strategy focuses on incentives. Electric cars are very profitable, and these profits will be shared with the salespeople who sell them. Marjorie and Stan know that money is very important, so they plan to meet with the salespeople to inform them that they will receive 30 percent higher commission on sales of electric cars when compared to what they earn for the sales of traditional vehicles.

Increased commission takes pressure off the salespeople because they can focus on individual sales rather than trying to push volume. They have more time to provide their customers with the information they need before making purchasing decisions. This creates a win/win situation because customers have more trust in the salespeople they are working with and the salespeople build lasting relationships that lead to repeat sales.

The biggest challenge for selling electric cars might be demographics. Four of the dealerships (#1, #2, #4, and #5) are located in affluent areas while one (#3) is in a socio-economically challenged area. This means salespeople at dealership #3 are at a disadvantage for selling cars due to lower household incomes. To eliminate this disadvantage, Marjorie gets Stan to agree to a 20 percent higher sales commission (added to the

30 percent increase) for all electric cars sold at dealership #3.

Over the next nine months, electric car sales more than double. The commissions from these sales, combined with those from traditional car sales, have resulted in 80 percent of the salespeople earning more money than they did in the same time period of the previous year, 15 percent earning about the same, and 5 percent earning less. Based on these figures, the HRM strategy is working as designed.

The above example shows how leaders use HRM to accomplish goals. Stan Watson, CEO, and Marjorie Newport, Human Resources Manager, work together to implement an HRM strategy that gets employees, specifically the salespeople, to accept change and move forward successfully; thereby creating a win/win situation for the company and the salespeople.

Now, let's move forward to a discussion on the relationship between HRM and hiring.

Hiring

It can be said with confidence that people are the most important resources in organizations. They dictate decision making processes and determine the culture and climate of workplaces, and they are the driving force behind any type of change. People with the right fit can take organizations to levels that were previously unattainable, but finding and hiring those people is often a challenging process that requires well-thought strategies. These strategies fall under the HRM umbrella, and they are usually developed and implemented by human resource professionals.

HRM hiring strategies are used in traditional organizations, such as manufacturing, and organizations are that on the cutting edge, such as companies focused on developing new technology. Quite simply, these strategies are ubiquitous because, regardless of the industry or type of business, people need to be recruited for employment. In terms of hiring workers, organizations without strategic plans are like powerless ships adrift on the water...always moving in different directions.

HRM Hiring strategies come in many different shapes and sizes depending on the need. For example, hiring college graduates in entry-level positions is much different than hiring senior executives. Entry-level employees are often hired based on expectations of what they can accomplish, while senior executives are hired based on what they have already accomplished. However, virtually every type of hiring strategy starts with some type of employee profile used as a baseline. This profile might not find the absolute best candidate, but it will eliminate those who do not possess the required skills, education, personality, and/or experience.

Some HRM hiring strategies require human resource professionals to use resources (often recruiters) outside of their own organizations....especially for high positions that require skills and experience that only a select few individuals possess. For example, a vice president of operations for a chain of grocery stores needs several years of multi-unit retail management experience that is preferably in the food industry. These requirements immediately eliminate most people, so the pool of potential candidates is limited. A local search might only yield a few prospects, but a national or international search greatly increases the number of qualified individuals and, ultimately, the chances of finding the best person for the job.

Unfortunately, finding the best person for the job is only half of the battle. This individual still has to accept the offer, so enticing her or him to accept needs to be part of the HRM hiring strategy. Companies want to get the most "bang for their buck" so they do not want to offer unreasonably high compensation, but they also want to avoid low-balling and risk losing a potentially good employee. The right offer requires research into what is a fair wage and benefit package. There also needs to be a plan for negotiation, since it is unlikely that an offer will be accepted without hesitation. Even a person who wants a job badly does not want to appear desperate, and HRM strategists need to take the potential for a counteroffer into account.

A different type of HRM hiring strategy stays away from any type of permanent employment. Instead, it focuses on temporary or contract workers to fill a need for designated or undesignated periods of time. Temporary employees typically do not have a date when their assignment will end while contract employees know in advance when their services will no longer be needed. This type of arrangement saves companies money in terms of benefits, but it also presents the risk that temporary or contract workers might leave for permanent employment.

Companies are hiring more temporary and contract workers today than they ever hired in the past. This trend has changed HRM hiring strategies to a short-term rather than long-term employment focus. These strategies are effective for accomplishing management hiring goals from a financial perspective, but there are not always for the better because some employees cannot adapt and leave their jobs for other employment. If the exiting of employees becomes a trend, then leaders of companies need to think about using different HRM hiring strategies.

Below is an example of an HRM hiring strategy implemented in the North American Division of Ridgeford and Associates, an international architectural firm.

Ridgeford and Associates

The North American division of Ridgeford and Associates has signed a contract with a national fitness company to design 21 stand-alone workout facilities in the southern half of the United States. The facilities will range in size from 40,000 – 100,000 square feet and will be located in 17 different states. The plan is to open them all within the next 18 months.

In order to complete a project of this size in the required time period, Ridgeford has to hire 15 additional architects. These architects will not be needed after the project is completed, so corporate managers at the firm decide to bring them in as contract employees. They believe this is the best way to meet the needs of their client without jeopardizing their profits after the work is done.

Human resources personnel implement an HRM strategy that offers contract work to people who meet the job posting requirements. The job posting is as follows:

- Contract architectural position for up to 18 months, renewed every 6 months.
- Minimum 7 years of experience in an architectural position.
- Architectural degree or equivalent education.
- Experience with commercial building design.
- Fitness building design experience is preferred.
- Relocation allowance.
- Wage based on experience.
- No benefits

The job posting is sent to a search firm that specializes in architectural design employees, with the need for filling the jobs being immediate. Within two days, the search firm has 32 potential candidates ready for phone interviews. Over the next two weeks, 21 of the candidates are brought into the North American Division of Ridgeford for in-person interviews. One week later, 15 architects have been hired as contract employees with 11 requiring a relocation allowance.

The above HRM strategy is an example of one used to hire contract employees. It meets the goals of Ridgeford by providing skilled workers on a temporary basis. This strategy does not require the same amount of time and effort as one designed to hire permanent employees because benefits and long-term employment are not taken into consideration, but it does show how hiring strategies work.

Let's move on to the next section that discusses the relationship between HRM and rewards.

Rewards

Rewards are very important to employees. In fact, they are often the most important reason why people work at an organization. If workers believe the rewards they receive are not worth the effort they put forth or the contribution they make, then they start to look elsewhere for employment.

The most obvious types of rewards are monetary in the form of wages, bonuses, benefits, and perks. Each of these is described below for easy understanding.

- *Wage* – Money paid to an employee for doing a job. It can be salary, hourly, job-based, or piece work-based, but it always equates to money paid for doing work.
- *Bonus* - Money paid in addition to a wage. It is added compensation that is above and beyond what is expected for work performed.
- *Benefit* - Non-wage compensation given to an employee in addition to a normal wage or bonus. It is often in the form of insurance (medical, dental, vision, life), retirement (pension, 401K), paid time off (vacation, holidays, personal days) or work-life balance (remote working, job-sharing).
- *Perk* – Non-wage compensation similar to a benefit, but not as defined or structured. It is often in the form of an extended courtesy such as free private parking spaces, childcare, concierges, shuttles, and event tickets.

The above rewards are tangible and have value, but intangible rewards also offer value to employees. These rewards do not necessarily have monetary value, but they are beneficial because they inspire employee motivation. They include thanks, praise, and recognition.

Public acknowledgement is one way to recognize employees. If they have done something positive that affects the community, then their accomplishments can be printed in local newspapers or shown on local television stations. If they have done something good that impacts their team or the entire organization, then they can be acknowledged in a meeting or talked about in an email.

Another recognition technique is done privately rather than publicly. It acknowledges employee accomplishments, but the acknowledgement comes in the form of encouragement whereby workers are encouraged to pursue their thoughts and ideas. This type of recognition is sometimes more important than any other because employees are allowed to take ownership of their jobs...which is very inspirational and motivational. In short, they are able to make decisions without micromanagement and restrictions that other employees are forced to endure.

There are many benefits for organizations that encourage the use of thanks, praise, and recognition. Employees typically become motivated, take pride in their work, perform at elevated levels, and have high job satisfaction. These benefits, however, might be better exemplified by discussing what happens when non-tangible rewards are non-existent in workplaces. Employees who are not recognized often become discouraged and disengaged. They start to take shortcuts while doing their jobs, pay less attention to details, and make mistakes. This type of behavior has a negative impact on profitability and can ultimately lead to the demise of organizations.

From an HRM standpoint, lack of non-tangible rewards causes retention strategies to erode to the point where they are no longer effective. Employees feel underappreciated and do not have the motivation necessary to complete tasks in the most effective and efficient manner. They lose interest in their jobs and begin to look for employment elsewhere. They also have nothing good to say about their employer when asked by people who are considering job openings.

In a nutshell, employees who receive praise and recognition build confidence as they engage themselves in their work. This engagement reduces their learning curves and encourages them to meet organizational goals by performing at high levels.

Below is an example of an HRM rewards strategy implemented at Harcourt Provision, a meat processing company with nine plants that supplies fresh pork to customers to the United States and Canada.

Harcourt Provision

Jeff Harcourt, CEO of Harcourt Provision, meets with his vice president of Human Resources, Lynn Corvallis, and informs her that he wants to implement a job-sharing program for workers at the corporate office. This change stems from responses to surveys asking employees about job satisfaction. Specifically, workers at the corporate office expressed a need to spend more time with their families. The vast majority of these workers were mothers who wanted to spend more time with their children, but other individuals also expressed interest. Job sharing will allow the increased family time to become a reality.

To accomplish the task set forth by Mr. Harcourt, Lynn composes an email and sends it to all corporate employees. She describes the new job-sharing benefit and tells them to fill out the attached form if they are interested in participating. Workers completing the form will be put into a pool and human resources personnel will determine which employees will be able to share jobs. Lynn explains that this process might take time because the job sharing situation must work for the employees and the company. In short, there must always be two qualified individuals who agree to split a job's responsibilities before it is considered for job sharing.

The job-sharing participation form is filled out by 160 employees. After a brief analysis, human resource personnel decide that 55 jobs meet the criteria so 110 employees are accepted into the program. The other employees are told to wait until a suitable arrangement is found, which is estimated to take about 90 – 120 days.

Within one month the job-sharing program is in full bloom, and an employee survey issued six months later shows a higher overall level of job satisfaction. This survey indicates the program has been successful, but it also provides added information that was previously unknown. Seventy-two of the 160 employees filling out the job sharing form were men; thereby contradicting management's belief that women would be by far the dominating gender. This finding is valuable for Harcourt Provision because it shows that men and women want better work-life balance. Based on this information, future HRM polices can focus on that want.

The above HRM strategy exemplifies the significance of intangible rewards to employees. It shows how management can use non-monetary incentives to help employees obtain something that is personally important to them. In this case, job-sharing was the objective, but work-life balance can be achieved in other ways such as remote working, in-house daycare, care for the aging, or being able to bring pets into the office. Regardless of the method, organizations need HRM rewards strategies in place to help meet the needs of their employees.

The next section focuses on the relationship between HRM and legal aspects of business.

Legal

HRM strategies are often designed for organizational growth and prosperity. They bring about high levels of employee motivation and build off the resulting productivity to help companies achieve accomplish goals and objectives. In a sense, these strategies take an offensive approach to competing for market share.

Growth-oriented HRM strategies have experienced success in many workplaces and leaders of all organizations should consider implementing them. However, HRM strategies that operate in defensive, rather than offensive, modes also need to be considered. These strategies defend organizations from internal and external forces that can damage or destroy them...and they often revolve around legal and regulatory aspects of business.

Internal forces that have the ability to cause harm often result from inappropriate employee behavior. Illegal and unethical worker actions can lead to long-lasting and expensive legal issues that are difficult to resolve. HRM strategies work well as preventative measures for these types of situations.

External forces that require defensive HRM strategies include situations where local, state, and federal government agencies have specific rules and regulations that must be adhered to. Organizations that fail to comply with these mandates risk monetary fines and, in worst-case scenarios, being forced to temporarily or permanently cease their business activities.

Human resources personnel also deal with forces that are both internal and external. Examples include contractual exchanges where employees, services, suppliers, and customers require written documentation that is governed by rules and regulations. New employees sign documentation indicating that they have received all necessary paperwork, suppliers sign letters of guarantee indicating their products and services meet specified requirements, and customers sign bills of lading indicating that everything on the paperwork was received in good condition.

Regardless of the type of paperwork signed, it is necessary to protect companies from lawsuits if contractual obligations are not met by one side or the other. This necessity often requires human resources personnel involvement so they can monitor contractual procedures, assure their completion, and maintain copies of all documentation. HRM strategies are very useful for moving these processes from start to finish.

HRM strategies are also useful for defending organizations from employee lawsuits that do not stem from contractual exchanges. Strategies can be employed that protect companies from employee theft of physical items, confidential information, or intellectual property. Unfortunately, employees in every type of business take things that are not rightfully theirs, and legal actions are required on behalf of the organizations that have been violated. HRM strategies determine where and when the benefits of legal action outweigh the costs and act accordingly.

HRM strategies protect organizations, but they also protect people...such as those in place to protect employees from the behavior of their coworkers and bosses. Harassment, discrimination, and coercion are all minimized or prevented using clearly designed workplace rules that designate appropriate and inappropriate behavior. Employees are protected from being discriminated against or harassed due to age, race, gender, disabilities, religion, sexual preference, and other factors. They are also protected from being forced to do things that they believe are legally, morally, or ethically wrong. In short, these types of HRM strategies are designed to safeguard employees from wrongful workplace behavior by providing management with the authority to discipline or terminate workers who act inappropriately.

HRM strategies geared toward legal and regulatory aspects of business usually require strict adherence to the rules within. This contradicts the soft-skill management approaches deemed necessary by some leadership gurus and consultants, but empathy and sensitively take a backseat to rigidity when employee legal action could result from rule deviance. Quite simply, legal strategies should be precisely followed if they are expected to work as planned.

Below is an example of an HRM legal strategy implemented at Randazzo Plastics, an injection molding company with three plants and 600 employees.

Randazzo Plastics

Eleven years ago, some of the Asian workers at one of the Randazzo plants complained that they were being harassed and made fun of by other employees. Coworkers made fun of their "slanted eyes" and mimicked their Chinese accents in a derogatory and mocking manner. Worse yet, management witnessed the wrongful behavior that was occurring and did little to correct the situation.

After several months of this intimidation and harassment, the Asians met with the vice president of operations, Rachelle Richardson, to file a complaint. Rachelle diffused the situation using employee/management meetings. Her actions prevented the Asian workers from taking any type of legal action against the company, but this incident made the president at Randazzo, Tony Ruez, realize that change was necessary. He met with the human resources manager, Terry Gage, and together they decided to implement an HRM strategy that focused on diversity.

Fast forward to the present and this HRM strategy is still in place. Part of the strategy involves mandatory diversity training for all employees. All non-management employees must go through a one day course that discusses the importance of diversity, provides real-world examples, and places the participants in role-playing situations where they need to react to potential problem situations.

Management training is more detailed and intense than non-management training since managers are expected to monitor the workplace for potential diversity issues. They must undergo a two three day course that takes place off-site to allow for better concentration on the subject matter. At the end of the training session, they must pass a written test indicating their understanding of the subject matter.

The above example shows how intangible HRM strategies work to prevent potentially damaging situations involving legal or regulatory aspects of business. This strategy takes a defensive approach to problem solving; thereby making it proactive rather than reactive.

Now, let's move to the next section that discusses the relationship HRM has with training.

Training

Training is used in the legal HRM strategy above, but it is by no means limited to a legal capacity. In fact, training occurs in virtually every aspect of business and that is why a section of this book is devoted to HRM training strategies.

Training has several functions. It helps workers understand important job aspects, brings about workplace awareness, teaches management skills, and aids employee professional development. Each of these is exemplified below for a better understanding.

- *Helps workers understand important job aspects*

  An example is on-the-job training so employees understand how to perform those jobs effectively and efficiently.

- *Brings about workplace awareness*

  An example is a course where employees are trained on how to react if an active shooter enters the workplace.

- *Teaches management skills*

  An example is a course for new supervisors designed to show them how to minimize and prevent employee conflicts.

- *Aids employee professional development*

An example is a course that shows employees how to prepare themselves for career advancement within the organization.

HRM Training encompasses many different aspects of organizations, but it is not limited to the examples above. In fact, it can be used for just about anything that requires the transfer of information between employees. Examples include training that assures employees understand the hierarchical structure, introduces them to new concepts and ideas, familiarizes them with their roles, and conveys management's expectations. This allows supervisors to focus on management roles without having to micromanage their employees.

It is no secret that organizations want educated workforces. HRM Training provides employees with new information that has great importance in the workplace. This information can be directly related to processes or procedures, such as learning a new email system, or it can be related to policies, such as sexual harassment.

Some training is generic while other training is specific. Generic training is general and it applies to a variety of different employees. Basic protocols and procedures are addressed, and the training covers a lot of material in a relatively short period of time. An example of generic training is new employee orientation that is designed for all employees hired by a company.

Specific training is precise and applies to a select group of employees. Detailed protocols and procedures are addressed, and the training covers a limited amount of material over a period that can last several days or weeks. An example of specific training is a microbiology course on the analysis of pathogenic bacteria that is designed for food processing plant laboratory technicians.

HRM training has a cost in terms of time and money, but it is expected to be advantageous in the long run. Below are some advantages of specific types of training.

- *On the job*

    This involves one employee teaching another how to do a job. The goal is for the employee being trained to learn by observation. An advantage of on the job training is employees learn from experienced people who are readily available to answer questions.

- *Web-based*

    This occurs is when employees go to specific websites to learn about designated aspects of their jobs. Sometimes a test is issued at the end, and a certain score is required for the employee to be considered competent in the subject matter. An advantage of web-based training is employees can usually do it at their convenience.

- *Webinars*

    Webinars are typically live web broadcasts that are conducted at a specific time and date. Employees accept invitations and log into virtual classrooms. An advantage of webinars is employees can ask questions to clarify any aspect of the training.

- *In-house*

  This is training within the organization that uses management personnel as facilitators. Employees gather at designated places during working hours and learn about specific aspects of their jobs. An advantage of in-house training is the trainers understand exactly what their organizations want employees to learn.

- *Consultant*

  This occurs when outside organizations are hired to do the training using their experienced instructors. An advantage of consultant based training is the facilitators understand the best ways to get people to learn because they are professional educators.

When implemented and maintained, HRM training strategies are beneficial for organizations. As mentioned earlier they help employees build job skills and prepare for higher-level positions. However, astute leaders know that they are also the least expensive and most efficient way to staff their organizations because the money spent is much less than that needed for filling positions via external recruiting. Additionally, the time needed for internal employees to adjust to the organizational culture is essentially none because they are already working in that culture. The same cannot be said when hiring external employees because they have to adjust to the way things are run and the way day-to-day business is conducted.

Obviously, all HRM training strategies do not experience success, but their presence creates opportunities that otherwise would exist. These opportunities are not always visible, such as the benefit of being able to learn from experienced managers, but they do show the need for companies to invest in training on a continuous basis.

Cultures in organizations with HRM training strategies progress into those that encourage employees to learn from their coworkers and share their existing knowledge with others. A win/win situation evolves where employees improve themselves and that improvement betters their organizations. Over time, it becomes the norm to develop, maintain, and enrich the knowledge base necessary for the growth and prosperity of employees and their employers.

Below is an example of an HRM training strategy implemented at Eschner Publishing, a digital and print book publisher with worldwide sales.

Eschner Publishing

Eschner Publishing has been in business for over 50 years and they take pride in the fact that they are firm believers in promoting from within. This belief requires them to have a strategy in place that grooms employees and prepares them for internal career advancement.

That strategy comes in the form of HRM training and it is operational throughout the organization.

The HRM training strategy at Eschner is based on educating the workforce about the way the company operates. Employees are encouraged to learn about their jobs, their supervisors' jobs, and the culture of their workplace through webinars, classroom experience, on the job training, and interaction with management.

The training is designed via the collaboration of management and human resource personnel in a relatively structured environment. This structure is not completely rigid or non-wavering, but it must be in place to maximize learning and show the company's commitment to internal promoting.

One type of training in the HRM strategy involves role-playing where workers assume a supervisory position and field "what if" type questions. This helps them understand how to react in situations they could potentially encounter once they are promoted. It has been shown to be quite beneficial over time because it prepares supervisors to act in ways that solve problems.

Another type of training involves one-on-one interaction with people in management. Employees are asked to designate a position that they would like to aspire to in the future, and they shadow the person currently in that position for several hours over a two-week period. They are then asked questions about what they observed, what they think was done right, and where they think improvements could be made. This program has been shown to be beneficial when employees move into supervisory roles by providing a glimpse of what management jobs are like on a daily basis.

The learning opportunity provided by Eschner inspires employees to do their best and motivates them to climb the corporate laddor. The success of the company has been attributed to the quality of the workforce, and that quality is due to the HRM training strategy that is in place.

The above example shows how HRM training strategies work to maximize employee efforts and prepare them for positions they might occupy in the future. When workers are aware that their company invests them, they are inspired to give back. These strategies are similar to intangible HRM rewards strategies because they are proactive rather than reactive so problems can be prevented from occurring.

Let's move forward to the next section that is often the most interesting to readers. This section explores HRM strategies used by organizations for employee relations.

Employee relations

Some people believe that relationships with employees are more important than anything else in business. This might or might not be true, but it can be said with certainty that employee relations are significant and contribute to organizational success.

HRM strategies involving employee relations are quite common in organizations because they provide the structure necessary for efficient operations. Policies in place typically address attendance problems, disciplinary actions, discrimination issues, employee rights, investigations, and ethics. Some of these policies, such as those involving discrimination and employee rights, tie in with HRM training strategies. An example is a policy for sexual harassment where it is mandatory that employees get trained in order to prevent the legal action that could potentially result from ignorance or negligence. This example shows how strategies for legal, training, and employee relations HRM are all combined. However, HRM employee relations strategies warrant a category of their own due to the generality involved. They focus on the entire strategy rather than specific aspects of it.

It is becoming increasingly more difficult to detect, deal with, and resolve employee relations issues. However, astute leaders understand that they must move past that difficulty. The process for doing this is often part of some type of HRM employee relations strategy. These strategies require managers to approach workforce diversity from a psychological point of view. They are trained in areas including active listening and communication with the goal being the reduction of workplace conflicts. This training, regardless of the depth or intensity, is not going to completely eliminate conflicts, but it can reduce them to a level where they can be effectively managed.

Conflict management is a big part of HRM employee relations strategies because it affects so many other issues in workplaces. If conflicts are reduced, then litigation, investigation, absenteeism, and disciplinary action become less frequent; thereby saving management time, money, and unnecessary stress.

It is important to mention that workplace conflict is not always bad. In fact, it is good in some instances because it can be used to develop new concepts and ideas. Positive conflict is referred to as functional because the related disagreements bring about change, and change is necessary for organizational growth and prosperity. Without some form of disagreement, companies would remain stagnant, get passed up by the competition, and eventually cease to exist.

Unfortunately, workplace conflict can also be quite detrimental...especially if employees refuse to focus on principle and will not budge from their position. Negative conflict is referred to as dysfunctional, and it can linger for years with no resolution. If it cannot be reduced or eliminated, then employee performance spirals downward and organizations suffer.

HRM employee relations strategies are designed to prevent dysfunctional conflict from occurring. Programs and policies are put in place to regulate employees' behavior and prevent speculative analysis or personal judgment from creating disharmony and chaos. An example is an attendance program set up to monitor the amount of unapproved time that employees miss from their jobs. Progressive disciplinary action, such as warnings and suspensions, take place as employees' missed time increases. This progressive action lets the offending employees know where they stand, prevents their coworkers from speculating about what type of punishment should be given to them, and avoids arguments over whether or not management favoritism plays a role. In short, a structured program is part of an HRM strategy that prevents employees from spending unnecessary time and effort arguing over what type of action should be taken when employees miss work.

Below is an example of an HRM employee relations policy at a Pontiac Footwear, a corporation that owns six shoe and boot manufacturing plants in Michigan, Ohio, and Illinois.

Pontiac Footwear

Pontiac Footwear has recently experienced several situations where an investigation was required to determine what happened. The worst of these situations involved an employee at the Novi, Michigan plant who threatened violence because he felt that he was disrespected by his supervisor. His supervisor vehemently denied this claim and he provided a very different explanation of why this issue occurred. Neither party would budge on his position so it was determined that an investigation was needed.

Unfortunately, the investigation that took place was inconclusive which made the supervisor and employee very unhappy because each firmly believed that his story was true and the other's story was falsified. The problem turned into a major conflict, so it was moved up the decision-making ladder until it reached Pontiac's board of directors. The board concluded that there was not enough information to make a fair decision, so the problem did not get resolved. However, the board did determine that the investigation that took place was poorly conducted as the following indicates:

- Facts are missing or inaccurate.
- Times and dates are missing or inaccurate.
- People who are involved are not interviewed.
- Interviews are not in-depth.
- Interviewers do not ask the right questions.

Based on the above, the board of directors charged human resources personnel with creating an HRM strategy for investigative report writing that would be mandatory for all employee conflicts, issues, or concerns including injury, theft, accidents, damage, harassment, intimidation, discrimination, and other incidents that occur in the workplace. These reports need to be written properly so all pertinent facts and information are documented.

Human resources personnel did a vast amount of research as well as talking to some external consultants. They developed a new program that takes all related factors into consideration while documenting detailed facts about the allegation. Information is typically gathered qualitatively and then used to make a quantitative analysis. For example, in the case of sexual harassment, the investigator needs to interview the accuser, accused, witnesses, and anyone else who knows something about the alleged incident.

In terms of interviewing, more is better because common denominators and general consensus can be extracted. This process of interviewing large numbers of people is known as qualitative information gathering. That information is then analyzed and a conclusion is drawn. For example, in a sexual harassment case, the conclusion is a decision that determines whether the accused is guilty or not guilty of the accusation. This decision-making process is quantitative because it provides an exact answer.

Below is a fictitious report issued by the human resources department that exemplifies the new program. Andover Industries is used as the company with the complaint occurring at their Holman Technology plant. The investigator and report writer is Donald Vanderhill.

An explanation of each section of the report writing process is provided. There are a total of 8 sections plus a review that also needs to be conducted before submitting the report.

Section 1 - Executive Summary

A discussion on the executive summary is somewhat premature at this point, but it is important to understand what it is and why it exists. Quite simply, an executive summary provides an image of the incident that took place for everyone that needs to know what happened. It is typically placed at the beginning of the report, but it is not written until the report is finished.

An executive summary is sometimes the most important aspect of an Investigative report because readers make decisions to stop or continue reading based on it. In short, it provides a snapshot of (1) the alleged behavior or wrongdoing, (2) the investigation of that alleged behavior or wrongdoing, and (3) the outcome of that investigation. If done correctly, an investigative summary is all the reader needs to obtain a basic understanding of the report and its findings.

Example

On November 23, 2018, Andover Industries received a complaint from a wheelchair-confined handicapped worker, Bob Mills, who claimed he was being harassed. Specifically, Bob said that Nick Williams called him "retard" and "Mr. Efficient" causing him to become embarrassed, angry, and demotivated.

On November 24, 2018, I, Donald Vanderhill, interviewed Mr. Mills and three different witnesses who supported his claims. Mathew Houghton, Trish Danielson, and Lyn Presnal all stated that this harassment has been ongoing for the past few months.

I, Donald Vanderhill. interviewed Mr. Williams on November 26, 2018, and he admitted he had made "a few comments" over the past week, but he denied making these comments for the past three months. He also stated that his comments were made jokingly and everyone viewed them as "light-hearted humor."

Based on my interviews, I substantiate Mr. Mills' claim of harassment. I recommend Mr. Williams be required to undergo the diversity acceptance training offered by our human resources department. I also informed Mr. Williams that a copy of this written report would be available for him by November 29, 2018.

The section following the Executive summary is known as the Opening.

Section 2 - Opening

Essentially, the opening section encapsulates important information regarding the investigation in a concise manner in terms that everyone can understand. The introduction to the Andover Industries' report is as follows:

Complaint identifier

CC441-10

Date of complaint

November 23, 2018

Accuser

Bob Mills

Accuser work information

Hire date – June 17, 2006
Position - Sander
Department – Finishing
Plant – Holman Technology
Supervisor – Roscoe Tillman
ID – 2113P

Accuser personal information

Address –
21455 Alexander St.
Avon Lake, OH 44012
DOB – 9/12/81
Phone - 216-221-4725
Work phone – Not applicable
Fax – Not applicable
Email - bob.mills@gmail.com
Work email – Not applicable
Social media – NA
Spouse – Erica Mills

Accused

Nick Williams

Accused work information

Hire date – October 22, 2015
Position - Grinder
Department – Finishing
Plant – Holman Technology
Supervisor – Roscoe Tillman
ID – 4229P

Accused personal information

Address –
29001 Redstone Court
Apt. 211
Cleveland, OH 44015
DOB – 8/17/93
Phone - 216-515--3756
Work phone – Not applicable
Fax – Not applicable
Email - nickwill93@hotmail.com
Work email – Not applicable
Social media –
Twitter - @nickwill93
Facebook - Nick Williams
Spouse – Not applicable

Investigator

Donald Vanderhill
Human Resource Manager
Holman Technology
3400 Richdale Rd.

Cleveland, OH 44109

Email – Donald.Vanderhill@andover.com

Work phone - 216-774-2300 X - 3775

Work fax - 216-774-2500

The opening provides some details that are not listed anywhere else in the investigative report. It provides information about the accuser, accused, and investigator for a basic understanding before moving into the rest of the report.

The next section is known as the incident, and it provides some specifics about the accusation and situation.

Section 3 - Incident

This is the section where the investigator describes what happened. The incident for the Andover Industries' report is as follows:

What is the accusation?

The accuser (an employee) alleges workplace harassment by the accused (a coworker).

Who is the accuser?

Bob Mills

Who supervises the accuser?

Roscoe Tillman

Who is accused?

Nick Williams

Who supervises the accused?

Roscoe Tillman

What are the specifics of the accusation?

> In reference to the Andover Industries' report, the incident is as follows:
>
> Bob Mills, a sander in the finishing department at the Holman plant, alleges that Nick Williams, a grinder in the finishing department at the Holman plant, has called him derogatory names on several occasions. Bob says that he put up with the harassment until it became unbearable; thereby affecting him psychologically and causing him to lose focus on his job responsibilities.

Now it is time to narrow the focus of the investigation, and this is done in the scope section.

Section 4 - Scope

This section of the report lists all steps in the investigation. The scope for the Andover Industries' report is as follows:

This investigation focuses on a complaint filed by an employee against a coworker. The alleged victim, alleged accuser, and three witnesses are interviewed to obtain details on the situation. Those details will be used to piece together what really happened and determine if the alleged complaint is legitimate.

Now, it is time to move into the interviews section. This is where most of the important information for the report is obtained.

Section 5 - Interviews

This section discusses every interview taken during the investigation. It essentially asks those involved to share their versions of the situation by discussing people involved, happenings, dates, times, statements, conversations, and behaviors. It is the most detailed section in the report, and it is useful for scrutiny or challenges that might arise later on.

The interviews for the Andover Industries' report were conducted in person by Donald Vanderhill, Human Resource Manager at Holman Technology. Donald asked the interviewees to provide their name, job, employee ID, and length of employment along with a detailed description of what happened on November 23, 2018.

On November 24, 2018, five employees were interviewed including Bob Mills, Nick Williams, Mathew

Houghton, Trish Danielson, Lyn Presnal, and Roscoe Tillman. Please note the following regarding these interviews:

- All interviews were voluntary.
- All interviews took less than ten minutes to complete.
- All statements provided were signed by the interviewees.
- None of the employees had to be re-interviewed.

The interviews are listed below.

Bob Mills (accuser)

I am Bob Mills, employee ID 2113P, and I work for Andover Industries as a Sander in the finishing department at the Holman plant. I have worked for Andover Industries for 12 years including 5 years at the Saddle Design and 7 years at Holman Technology.

On November 23, 2018, at about 1:00 pm, Nick William made fun of me by calling me a "retard" due to the fact that I am confined to a wheelchair and need help maneuvering when performing my job duties. Specifically, another employee needs to operate a lift when I need to sand machinery at levels that I cannot reach from the ground. I was offended by this and told nick that I am very capable of doing my job to the satisfaction of my boss, Roscoe Tillman, but all he did was smirk and say "you are right, so I will call you Mr. Efficient."

Nick has made fun of me in the past, but this time I was very upset and decided to file a harassment complaint with human resources at the Holman plant. I filed the complaint because I was so mad that I could not focus on my job responsibilities and believed something needed to be done to stop Nick from insulting me.

Nick Williams (accused)

I am Nick Williams, employee ID 4229P, and I am employed at the Andover Industries' Holman Technology plant as a Finisher in the Finishing Department. I have worked for Andover Industries for 3 years at the Holman plant.

On November 23, 2018, at about 1:00 pm, I made fun of Bob by calling him "retarded," and he went to human resources to complain about my comment. The fact of this matter is that I was completely joking, and Bob knew I was joking. We kid back and forth all the time, so I don't know why this time is such a big deal. He has said stuff to me in the past, but I have never filed a complaint. This situation has been blown way out of proportion by Bob and everyone else. This company is way too sensitive about kidding around and, in this situation, a "mountain is being made out of a molehill."

Mathew Houghton (witness)

I am Matt Houghton, employee ID 2006P, and I work for Andover Industries as a Sander in the Finishing Department at the Holman plant. I have worked for Andover Industries for 14 years at Holman Technology.

On November 23, 2018, at about 1:05 pm I witnessed Nick Williams call Bob Mills a "retard." Bob became upset and said something to Nick that I could not hear. He then looked even angrier and said he was going to Human Resources to file a complaint.

Trish Danielson (witness)

I am Trish Danielson, employee ID 9225L, and I work for Andover Industries as Inventory Control Specialist in the Inventory Department at the Holman plant. I have worked for Andover Industries for 4 years at Holman Technology.

On November 23, 2018, at about 1:00 pm I heard Nick Williams call Bob mills a "retard," causing Bob to get mad. Bob told Nick he did not want to be called names and abruptly walked away. I did not know where Bob was going, but he was moving quickly. After Bob left, Nick thought the situation was funny.

Lyn Presnal (witness)

I am Lyn Presnal, employee ID 9811Q, and I work for Andover Industries as a Quality Assurance Technician in the Quality Department at the Holman plant. I have worked for Andover Industries for 2 years at Holman Technology.

On November 23, 2018, at about 1:00 pm I witnessed Nick Williams call Bob mills a "retard." I did not hear Bob's response, but he said something back to Nick while Nick laughed at him. Bob then said he was going to human resources and stormed off.

Roscoe Tillman (supervisor of accused and accuser)

I am Roscoe Tillman, employee ID 1744P, and I am employed at the Andover Industries' Holman Technology plant as the Finishing Supervisor in the Finishing Department. I have worked for Andover Industries for 28 years including 6 years at the Prevention Controls facility and 22 years at Holman Technology.

I did not witness the situation between Bob Mills and Nick Williams, but Bob told me in the past that he would prefer not to work with Nick. When I asked him why he did not want to work with Nick, he said it was due to "personality differences" that did not involve the job. I tried to separate Bob and Nick as much as possible, but they work in the same department, sometimes on the same jobs, so keeping them apart all the time is not practical.

Now that the problem has been defined and the witnesses' accounts of what transpired have been documented, it is time to move forward. The next section analyses the information available so a decision can be made about the innocence or guilt of Nick Williams.

Section 6 - Analysis

I, Donald Vanderhill, conducted the entire analysis.

I found that all three of the witnesses' stories corroborated; thereby determining that their stories must all be accurate. This finding of accuracy is further supported by the fact that all three witnesses have never been written up or disciplined for anything while employed at Andover Industries. In short, they are employees in good standing with the company.

I also believe that there have been problems between Bob Mills and Nick Williams based on my interview with their supervisor, Roscoe Tillman. He tried to keep these two apart, but their separation is not in the best interest of Andover Industries, so his decision to have them work together in certain instances is justified. Roscoe only has one write-up during his employment at Andover, and that was for attendance issues in 1994, so his testimony is further supported due to his good standing with the company.

The only story I found to be false is that from Nick Williams because he was the only person with this version of the story. Nick does not believe his behavior was offensive or abusive, but he is clearly wrong based on the no harassment policy that Andover Industries has had in place since 1995. Nick Williams has two previous write-ups documented on his record in the 3 years that he has worked here. He unsuccessfully argued that he was not guilty in both instances; thereby raising questions about his truthfulness in this situation.

Section 8 - Conclusion

Based on my analysis, I find that Bob Mills' allegation that Nick Williams harassed him is true. Mr. Williams' behavior fits the definition of harassment as defined in the Anderson Industries' employee handbook, and there is no "grey" area that warrants discussion.

This report and its findings will be passed to Henrietta Kowalski, Director of Human Resources for Anderson Industries, and she will decide what type of disciplinary action, if any, will be taken against Nick Williams.

Section 8 - Recommendations

The findings of this investigation show that harassment exists in the workplace at Anderson Industries. We should benefit from this incident by incorporating measures that will help prevent harassment in the future. I recommend mandatory diversity training for all employees at least once per year. This training will highlight the differences between employees and offer ways to help our workers accept those differences. Additionally, question and answer sessions should be available for employees who are unsure of what is expected of them in terms of diversity acceptance.

Review

Regardless of how good the report might be, it is critical to review it before submitting it to others. The following should be considered:

- Were any pertinent facts left out? Is anything missing? Were all "rocks uncovered and looked under?"
- Were all witnesses interviewed? Did anyone else see what happened? If so, can they be located and interviewed?
- Is the conclusion bias? Is the investigative report writer honest and sincere? Is there any type of discrimination?
- Were all relevant factors taken into account? Did the accuser have a reason to go after the accused? Was the accused targeted?
- Were the circumstances taken into account? Did the accused or have mental health problems, excessive stress, physical illness, or something else that caused them to do what they did?
- Are there any spelling or grammatical errors? Do these errors make the writer look careless? Should the report be edited by a professional?
- Does the report need to be reviewed by attorneys? Is the report safe from a legal standpoint? Is it possible that a lawsuit could result?

- Is the report stored in a secure place? Is it only assessable to authorized people? Can unauthorized people view it?

All of the above questions need to be considered in order to write a well-written, unbiased, and accurate report. A thorough review could prevent mistakes that end up leading to other problems...including legal action.

The above example shows how an HRM strategy works for employee relations. It shows how a report should be written to avoid missing important details, and it meets the requirements set forth by the board of directors.

Absenteeism

Absenteeism is defined as employees' unscheduled absence from their jobs. The key word here is "unscheduled." Scheduled absences can be planned for in advance, and this helps avoid some of the potential problems that might occur during an employees' time off. However, there is very little time to plan for unscheduled absences, and the necessary resources might not be available on a moment's notice.

Leaders in organizations are not naive enough to think employees are going to be at work on every scheduled day. They expect workers to miss some time because they are not feeling well or want to attend to personal matters that conflict with the times they are supposed to be at work. This behavior is acceptable and does not present a problem...unless it becomes excessive.

When absenteeism becomes excessive, it is a major headache for organizations. If employees do not show up for work, then their jobs need to be performed by other people. If no other people are available, then those jobs simply do not get done. This creates difficult and stressful situations for workers and managers, and it occurs far too often in some workplaces.

Unscheduled absence can be intentional or unintentional as shown in the following examples:

Intentional absenteeism

Manny comes home from work on Wednesday night and finds an envelope in his front door. As a surprise, one of his best friends leaves two baseball tickets to the Atlanta Braves home opening game that starts Thursday at noon. Manny is thrilled, and he texts his friend that he will be at the game.

The next morning, Manny calls his employer and tells them that he will not be at work. He says he has some "personal business" that he needs to attend to, and he will return on Friday.

Manny's decision to miss work in order to go to the baseball game is an example of intentional absenteeism.

Unintentional absenteeism

Juanita and George are married with two children under the age of five. They both work full-time jobs, and her husband frequently travels. This week he is away on a business trip.

George's business trips are normally not a problem for Juanita because drops her children off at daycare in the morning before going into work. However, this morning she wakes up to find her daughter vomiting. This child will not be able to go to daycare today and Juanita is the only person who can care for her. She calls work and tells them that she will not be in today due to a sick child.

Juanita's decision to miss work in order to take care of a sick child is an example of unintentional absenteeism.

In the view of an employer, Juanita's decision is much more legitimate than Manny's for missing work. However, regardless of the intent, unscheduled absences do not allow organizations to plan for handling missing employee's work that needs to be completed. For this reason, it is important to understand the causes of absenteeism so attempts can be made to eliminate them and minimize absences on scheduled workdays.

It is virtually impossible to list every cause of absenteeism due to the fact that every employee is unique. However, the following are some major causes of these unscheduled absences:

Stress

Work-related stress can lead to mental and physical health problems if it is not dealt with in some manner. Employees use a variety of different techniques to deal with stress including yoga, exercise, meditation, relaxation, massage, and therapy. However, workers also deal with stress by not showing up for work...and this is why it is a cause of absenteeism.

Family care

Family care has changed considerably since the 1960s. Mothers used to stay home to take care of children while fathers worked to financially support the family. However, this has changed. Today many, if not most mothers, are employed in some capacity. Children go to daycare and are picked up after the parent's workdays are finished.

The dual-income family works well financially for many families, but this arrangement poses a problem when children get sick. One of the parents needs to stay home to care for the child, and this means that he or she needs to miss work. Although this absence is unintentional, it is still unscheduled and therefore classified as absenteeism.

Family care absenteeism does not end with care for children. Employees today are part of the "sandwich generation" where they need to help young children and aging parents. When a parent needs assistance, one of their children needs to miss work to provide the necessary care...and the end result is an unscheduled absence. So, the same people who miss work for their children can also miss work for their parents.

In short, family care today is a major cause of absenteeism based on dual-income households and the needs of various relatives. This will continue to present a challenge as long as working couples have young children and aging parents.

Bereavement

An old saying goes, "two things people have to do during life are die and pay taxes." The taxes part is debatable...but the part about dying is an absolute fact.

When people die, friends and family need time to grieve over the loss. However, it is difficult to specify how long employees should mourn because everyone is different. Some workers need more time than others and therefore end up missing more days of work. Since this missed time is unscheduled, it is considered absenteeism.

Illness

Essentially, illness can be physical or mental. Physical illness can be as simple as the common cold or as serious as terminal cancer. Mental illness often involves some type of depression, but it can also involve issues such as paranoia or schizophrenia.

It is not uncommon for employees to become physically ill. Their illnesses often require them to miss work, and the number of days they are absent depends on the time required for healing.

Management expects employees to miss some time at work due to physical illness, but that time is not scheduled in advance and is therefore deemed absenteeism.

Mental illness is not as common as physical illness, but it does affect employees in every type of workplace. This illness often requires people to miss work, and they are not able to return until their conditions are cured or controlled.

Management typically does not expect employees to miss work due to mental illness, but they do understand that it does occur. However, the time missed is unscheduled and is therefore considered absenteeism.

Bullying

Employees who are bullied by coworkers might choose to stay home rather than come to work and take the abuse. This type of situation is unfortunate because bullying can lead to depression and long-term negative effects. Bullying might not be one of the most common causes of absenteeism, but it is one of the most important due to other problems that can result.

Poor supervision

Poor supervision is a problem in many organizations, but only the more severe cases result in absenteeism. Employees simply cannot bear to see their supervisors, so they decide to call in sick. They become overwhelmed with negative thoughts and choose to avoid the situation rather than deal with bosses that they disdain.

Workload

Workloads can be so excessive that employees choose to stay home rather than go to work. Ironically, the absenteeism resulting from workloads is often an indirect consequence of other absenteeism. This is because employees miss work and their coworkers have to do their jobs. Those coworkers then have much larger workloads, so they also decide to not show up for work. Unfortunately, this cycle can repeat itself until the overworked employees burn out and permanently leave the organization.

Working conditions

Working conditions have a big impact on absenteeism. Workplace temperature, sanitary conditions, and ergonomics all play a role in determining if employees will show up for work.

Cold temperatures create discomfort and cause workers to lose focus. All they think about is getting to a warmer environment, and that in itself is enough to make them not show up for work.

Unsanitary conditions result in mental disgust for some employees. They would rather be home than in a dirty workplace and decide not to come to work.

Dimly lit areas cause eye strain. This makes it difficult to complete work and causes headaches. Due to the pain, employees call in sick.

Travel

Some jobs require employees to travel. This is not a problem unless the travel becomes excessive. Employees do not want to constantly be on the road because they miss out on many aspects of their personal lives. When they finally get home, they want to spend time with family and friends rather than going right into the office...so they tell their employer that they will not be in. This is understandable, even in the eyes of some employers, but it is still considered absenteeism.

Personal reasons

There are times when people do not go to work for personal reasons. They choose to attend a daytime sporting event, catch a matinee movie, go on a day trip with a friend, or just relax in front of the television at home. This is also known as "playing hooky," and it happens in workplaces all over the world.

Employers typically do not view personal reasons as legitimate excuses for missing work. However, they realize that employees are going to "play hooky," and there is not much that can be done about it. This form of absenteeism will likely occur in some capacity as long as people work for organizations.

Injury

Injuries are legitimate reasons for missing work. When employees are hurt, they cannot perform certain aspects of their jobs, and therefore need to be off work.

As far as employers are concerned, there two basic types of injuries, work-related and non-work related. Work-related injuries result from accidents that occur on the job. Workers' compensation pays for the employees' time missed because the injury occurred while working. This is bad for the employer for two different reasons because (1) their insurance premiums increase due to the claims and (2) their employees are not able to perform their jobs.

Non-work related injuries result from accidents that do not occur on the job. Employers are not required by law to compensate employees who are not injured at work...although some provide short-term and long-term disability benefits. Employers save money by not paying injured employees, but they still lose because these individuals are not able to perform their jobs.

Employers realize that injuries are going to occur. However, these claims can be abused. Workers who do not want to come back to work can often get doctors to extend their excused absence regardless of whether or not they are healed.   If this happens, then absenteeism is even more costly to employers...especially if workers' compensation is being paid to the injured employees.

Other employment

Some employees miss work because they are working other jobs. This is usually not acceptable to employers...and some even consider it grounds for termination. However, regardless of the rules in place, other employment is a cause of absenteeism that occurs in many workplaces.

Job searches

This involves missing work to (1) look for another job or (2) interview at another organization. Obviously, most employers would frown upon this because they are on the verge of losing employees...and those employees might be going to competitors. However, in reality, missing work for job searching is fairly common because interviews are typically conducted during normal working hours.

Transportation

Most people need some type of transportation to get to their jobs. If that transportation is not available, then they are unable to show up for work. This type of problem is more common for employees who rely on public transportation, but personal vehicles also break down.

Transportation issues are usually beyond the control of employees. However, they are still considered unscheduled absences and a cause of absenteeism.

Excessive hours

Employees who work too many hours sometimes miss work just to get some personal time away from the job. For example, a production plant might be working seven days a week. After two or three weeks without a day off, employees decide to stay home and rest instead of going into work. This rest is obviously justified, but it is considered absenteeism.

Strange hours

Some employees miss work because they work strange shifts or hours. For example, third shift employees might never get to see their families or friends, so they decide to not come into work in order to attend special events in their lives. This type of absenteeism is more likely to happen to employees who work when most people are at home or out socializing.

Religion

Leaders in organizations are beginning to realize that employees need time off for designated religious occasions that might not be recognized by the government.   However, this type of management thinking is in its infancy, and it will be a while before employees are excused for the days they consider sacred. Until that time, workers will not show up for work for religious reasons, and their unscheduled absences will be considered absenteeism.

Drugs and alcohol

Substance abuse is an issue in many workplaces, and this is likely to continue as long as drugs and alcohol are readily available to employees.   In some cases, management is required by law to allow employees time to deal with their addictions...and these absences are not part of absenteeism since they are scheduled. However, hangovers and other substance related aftermath are considered absenteeism, and they will likely never be accepted as legitimate by leaders of organizations.

Attitude

Attitude is a major cause of absenteeism. Employees who have negative attitudes about their place of work tend to show up less frequently than coworkers with positive attitudes. Attitude is about perception...and perception truly is reality.

Age

Age is also a cause of absenteeism. Typically, younger workers miss time because they are out socializing or having fun. Older employees often miss time for health concerns or family situations.

Younger and older employees miss work for different reasons, but all of those reasons result in unscheduled absences.

Seniority

Long-term employees sometimes feel a sense of entitlement when in terms of taking unscheduled time off from work. They have been with the organization for a long time and believe their seniority gives them the right to be absent without notice. Unfortunately, this is still considered absenteeism...and it requires other employees to do extra work.

Boredom

Repetition makes jobs mundane. Employees lose the motivation to work after repeating the same task throughout their workday, and this leads them to take unscheduled days off work. In short, boredom is a cause of absenteeism because it does not provide employees with challenges.

Some causes of absenteeism are specific to certain groups of employees such as immigrants. These include:

Family businesses

Some employees miss work because they need to work at seasonal family businesses. For example, they might need to leave to help their family work in the fields during harvesting periods.

Absenteeism caused by family businesses can be a big problem for organizations if too many workers leave at the same time. The mass exodus of employees can cripple productivity and even force some organizations to cease operations.

Unrecognized holidays

Similar to religious occasions, some holidays are not recognized by organizations in the United States. Examples include Cinco de Mayo, Greek Easter, and Rosh Hashanah.

Management is beginning to realize that employees need time off for designated holidays, but it will be a while before they are formally excused. Until that time, workers will not show up for work on days they consider holidays, and their unscheduled absences will be considered absenteeism.

Homeland visits

Some employees miss work because they go back to their homelands to visit friends and family. These visits are very important to these workers, and they leave regardless of whether their absences are approved by management.

This type of absenteeism is difficult to prevent because employees have strong ties to people from their countries of origin.

Absenteeism negatively affects employers and employees in a variety of different ways. Some of the major ways include:

Wages and benefits

In many cases, especially those involving workers' compensation, absent employees still receive wages and benefits until they are able to return to work. In some cases, these payouts can go on for years...and possibly even the rest of the employees' lives.

Overtime

As noted earlier, absent employees leave work behind that still needs to be done by coworkers. Those coworkers need to work longer hours to complete the designated tasks, and they are paid overtime for those hours.

Training

Absent workers sometimes need to be replaced by new employees. These new employees need to be trained...and that training has a cost associated with it.

Administrative

Many people are not aware that there are administrative costs for managing absenteeism. For short-term absences, letters need to be sent to the offenders detailing disciplinary action. For long-term absences such as those involving workers' compensation, massive amounts of paperwork need to be filled out...and this takes time and resources. Additionally, meetings need to be conducted with insurance companies, medical providers, and attorneys to discuss specifics of the case.

In short, absenteeism impacts the bottom lines of organizations. This impact is never good, and it can lead to some companies permanently shutting down.

Below is an example of an HRM absenteeism strategy implemented by Rodriquez Foods, a manufacturer of Hispanic food for retail and foodservice establishments with five manufacturing plants located in Texas, Louisiana, and New Mexico.

Rodriquez Foods

This HRM absenteeism strategy consists of three parts and it incorporates portions of the hiring and rewards strategies discussed in this book. However, absenteeism is such an important aspect of business that it warrants being in a category of its own.

The first part of this HRM strategy starts at the beginning by modifying hiring practices. Effective hiring practices are likely the best way to prevent absenteeism because (1) they prevent problem employees from entering the workplace and (2) they prevent employees from becoming problem employees.

The following are requirements before employees can be hired to work at Rodriquez:

Reference checks

Past employers must be called to determine if potential employees have a history of absenteeism. It is illegal for employers to divulge certain facts about past employees, but they can release attendance records if policies were in place. This allows Rodriquez to find out if potential employees were terminated for absenteeism related reasons.

Attendance emphasis

The importance of showing up for work must be stressed before hiring. Discussion must take place regarding absenteeism and the attendance policies in place...including disciplinary actions for violations.
This makes it clear to employees that they are needed on the job and expected to show up when they are scheduled.

All employees must sign a document stating that they understand the importance of attendance and will follow company mandated attendance policies.

The second part of the HRM attendance strategy takes place after employees are hired and it involves rewards. Rewards are a good way to prevent absenteeism because they provide goals and motivation for employees to show up for work.

There are several different types of rewards including:

Awards

Awards are certificates that commend good employee attendance. They are motivational because employees are recognized in front of the entire organization.

Incentive pay

Employees are paid for good attendance. In other words, the incentive for reducing absenteeism is a monetary reward. These rewards are accumulated monthly and paid out in the form of a quarterly bonus. Details of the payout are located in the employee handbook.

Lotteries

Workers with good attendance are also randomly rewarded. These individuals are entered in monthly lotteries with cash prizes that go to the selected winners. Details of the lottery process are located in the employee handbook.

The rewards are based on the employee attendance policy that is in place. This policy is detailed in the employee handbook, but it essentially works by issuing points for unscheduled or unexcused absences. These points accumulate over time and workers who reach a specified number are progressively disciplined...up to the point where they are terminated for extreme absenteeism.

The third and final part of the HRM attendance policy is job rotation where employees move from job to job until they learn how to do them all. This rotation prevents absenteeism by (2) reducing the boredom of performing only one job and (2) empowering employees because they are more involved in the operation of the organization. IT also benefits the company because employees know how to do each other's jobs when someone is absent; thereby reducing mistakes and saving time in terms of training.

The above HRM strategy is designed to prevent absenteeism before it starts to become an issue. It educates employees on the importance of them showing up for work and rewards them for good attendance.

The next section focuses on the relationship between HRM and employee performance.

Performance

Leaders of organizations are intrigued with performance because they are consistently plagued with the problem of getting their employees to perform at peak levels. Workers can be motivated to perform optimally for short amounts of time, but it is very difficult to maintain that level for prolonged periods.

Since employees do not always perform to the best of their abilities, they need to be evaluated to see whether or not their performance meets pre-determined criteria and, if not, what can be done to improve it. This evaluation is known as a performance review and it takes place in organizations all over the world.

Organizations can employ several different types of review strategies, but they need to be categorized for a better understanding of their importance in the workplace. Below are some specific types of reviews that occur in organizations along with real-world examples for clarity and comprehension.

Supervisor

This type of review typically involves a one-on-one encounter with the supervisor and employee. The supervisor completes a written evaluation with questions related to performance, including strengths and weaknesses, and discusses it with the employee. The employee has the right to challenge any aspect of the supervisor's evaluation, and disputes that cannot be resolved are taken to a higher level of management.

Once the review is agreed upon by both parties, it becomes a permanent part of the employee's file.

The major advantage of the supervisor review is efficiency. Supervisors typically understand the job responsibilities and expectations of their subordinates. Their familiarity allows them to easily answer most of the review questions, and they are able to make a fairly accurate assessment of employee performance in a reasonable amount of time.

Organizational example

Scott is the production manager in a juice manufacturing plant. He reports to the plant manager Jennifer, and today is his annual review.

Jennifer understands Scott's job responsibilities well because she was the production manager prior to being promoted to plant manager. She thinks he does a good job professionally and also likes him personally. Scott also just finished a project for her that was very successful.

Jennifer answers the review questions on the designated form with no difficulty and then meets with Scott to discuss the details of her evaluation. Scott believes the review is fair and accurate, and it becomes a part of his permanent employee file. This review is simple to conduct and takes less than one hour to complete.

In short, Jennifer understands Scott's job quite well and likes him on a personal and professional level. This allows her to accurately appraise him in a short period of time.

Self

Self-reviews involve employees rating themselves on pre-designated criteria established by the organization. Employees identify their strengths and weaknesses in a variety of areas including performance and work relationships, and they suggest areas where they can improve and grow professionally.

This evaluation can be done using essay responses or a Likert scale. Essays provide a detailed account of employee perceptions, while Likert scales have a range, for instance from 1 to 5, which gives a quantifiable score.

An advantage of self-reviews is that employees gain awareness of their actions and their relationships with others, and this leads to increased accountability.

Organizational example

Ralph works as a bartender at a restaurant that is part of a national chain. He has his six-month review scheduled for today, and corporate management has just informed him that he needs to do a self-evaluation for this appraisal.

Ralph evaluates himself using a Likert scale provided by the company. He rates himself between 1 (poor) and 10 (excellent) for the 20 different categories that assess his performance, growth, and work relationships.

Ralph's scores indicate he has a good relationship with his immediate supervisor, but he needs to improve in three different areas. Because he found the areas for improvement on his own, he is motivated to take accountability and make the necessary changes. These changes should come fairly easy due to the positive association he has with his manager.

Peer

Peer reviews are conducted by team members or coworkers, rather than by the employees themselves or their supervisors. Specifically, peers are asked to anonymously rate the performance of their coworkers. These comments are usually given the supervisor of the employee being reviewed, but sometimes they are also shared directly with the employee.

An advantage of peer reviews is that they are often perceived as more fair than reviews conducted by a supervisor because multiple minds provide a more accurate judgment of performance. Additionally, peer reviews are valuable to the workplace in general because they create a culture that encourages feedback and teamwork.

Organizational example

William works as a teller at a bank. His review is scheduled for today, and it will be conducted by his peers. Seven other tellers have shared their opinions about William's performance with Joan, the bank manager.

Joan gathers the information and finds that William is well-liked by employees and customers, but he has trouble arriving at work on time. Joan was not aware of this because William starts earlier than her, but she makes sure she shares this information with him.

William is happy that others perceive him as an excellent customer service person. However, he also realizes that his tardiness is an issue because everyone sees it as an area where he needs to improve. Based on his coworkers' analysis, William begins to leave his home earlier in the morning to make sure he arrives to work on time.

In summary, William perceived his peers' critique as fair and legitimate because other tellers had similar comments regarding his performance.

360

This review uses self-analysis, peer assessment, supervisor feedback, and subordinate evaluation (if applicable) for the appraisal. It assesses self-perception (from employees being reviewed), performance (from supervisors), character (from peers), and leadership skills (from subordinates).

The major advantage of the 360 review is that it gives a complete picture of employee performance based on input from multiple sources.

Organizational example

Wanda is a supervisor at an automotive supplier. Her review is today, and her company has decided to a 360 appraisal. The Human resources manager meets with Wanda, her boss, three other supervisors, and three of her direct reports.   The appraisal process takes place over the next three days, and the various evaluations do a wonderful job portraying Wanda's performance.   Without the input of these different employees, the review would not have as detailed or complete.

In short, Wanda's job performance was clearly depicted due to the diversity of the employees who participated in her evaluation

MBO

MBO is an acronym for "Management By Objectives" that was first popularized in 1954 by management guru Peter Drucker. It involves employees and supervisors working together to establish goals that need to be achieved in a certain time frame. The thinking behind this type of appraisal is that employees who are involved in setting their own goals will be more motivated to accomplish them.

The advantage of MBO reviews is that it is easy to establish success or failure at the next review. Employees are successful if the goals have been achieved, and they have failed if the goals have not been achieved.

Organizational example

Katrina is a sales representative for a line of cosmetics, and her boss Patrick decides to do an MBO evaluation at her mid-year review. Patrick asks Katrina what goals she would like to set for herself. She knows she needs to sell $400,000 worth of product to get a bonus, but she wants to do better. She sets a goal of $500,000 in sales, and Patrick agrees.

For the next six months, Katrina works very hard. She wants to achieve her goal because she established it, and this makes her feel more personally involved. At her year-end review, she achieves her goal of $500,000 in sales, and Patrick rewards her with a raise in her base pay.

In summary, Katrina's involvement in setting a work-related goal during her mid-year review motivated her to achieve that goal. By her year-end review, she achieved the goal she established for herself, and Patrick rewarded her for being successful.

Scale

This is a less popular type of review than most of the others because the management has to spend time and effort developing the questions and rating scale that will be used. Essentially, it is a grading system that assesses a variety of aspects related to employee performance including job skills, communication, collaboration, and understanding. Employees need to meet a minimum score, similar to that in education, in order for their review to be considered successful. Those who do not meet the minimum score are put on a performance improvement plan.

The advantage of scale reviews is they are custom made for organizations. This gives management the ability to ask questions that are specific to a particular workplace.

Organizational example

John is a salesperson at a mortgage company, and his review is being conducted using the scale method. John has sold the second most mortgages in the company, proving that he understands his job and is productive. He is also well-liked by employees and customers and works well with others on team projects. John easily meets the minimum performance score, and this means that he is successful as a salesperson.

John's job skills, communication, collaboration, and understanding help him achieve a very good score in his review, and this indicates that he is competent in his position.

Below is an example of an HRM performance strategy implemented by Namath Controls, an automotive parts distributor with warehouses in Florida, Nevada, and Minnesota. This strategy combines a few different types of reviews for an objective view of an employee's performance.

Namath Controls

Over the past decade, Namath Controls has experienced rapid expansion in the automotive parts distribution business. Their sales have more than doubled, and this has been good for stockholders and the company's bottom line. However, the downside to this expansion has been their ability to maintain good employees. They seem to lose workers who do a good job while holding on to subpar employees.

After some extensive analyses, the CEO at Namath has determined that the current performance measurement is weak. A system is in place, but it is rather simple because it only involves supervisor perception. Essentially, supervisors evaluate their employees' efforts and give raises based on that evaluation. There is no documented feedback, good or bad, and there is no type of improvement plan administered to underperforming workers. This means good workers are not told they are doing well and sub-par workers continue to work for the company even though their contributions are less than acceptable.

Based on this analysis, the CEO tells the human resource department to develop an evaluation strategy that is more effective than the current program.

Human resources personnel do some research and come up with a three-stage evaluation strategy. They plan to implement this strategy after it has been reviewed and found acceptable by the CEO.

The first stage of the strategy involves peer-reviewed evaluation. Employees will be required to evaluate the other workers in their departments for ability, effort, and teamwork as shown below.

> *Ability* – Rate the employee in terms of job skills for doing his or her job effectively and efficiently.

> *Effort* – Rate employee in terms of effort put forth to do his or her job.

> *Teamwork* – Rate the employee in terms of working with others in a group setting.

For each of the above ratings, a 1-5 Likert scale will be used with grading as follows:

1 = excellent
2 = good
3 = average
4 = needs improvement
5 = poor

In addition to the above grading, an area will be provided for an explanation of why the employee was given the selected score.

The second stage of the strategy involves supervisor evaluation. The supervisor will complete a written performance evaluation with the employee's strengths and weaknesses. Unlike the peer-reviewed evaluation, and Likert rating scale will not be used. The employee rating will be marked as "acceptable" or not "acceptable" with an area provided for an explanation of the reasoning for the selected score. For every unacceptable mark, there must be a suggestion for improvement.

After the supervisor stage, the third and final stage will take place. In this stage, the employee meets with human resources personnel and is informed of the evaluation findings. Low peer ratings (an average score of below 3.0) and unacceptable supervisor marks require an improvement plan. This plan is developed by the employee and human resources personnel; thereby allowing the employee to take ownership of the improvements that need to take place.

The employee has the right to challenge human resources personnel on any aspect of his or her evaluation, and disputes that cannot be resolved will be taken to a higher level of management. Once the review is agreed upon by both parties, it becomes a permanent part of the employee's file.

The above HRM strategy exemplifies a three-part performance strategy that is based on more than a simple supervisor review. It provides a broad analysis of how employees perform and requires an improvement plan for those whose work is found to be unacceptable. This meets the objectives of the CEO while retaining the good employees and flushing out the sub-par workers.

Now, let's move to the final section that examines the relationship between HRM and safety.

Safety

Workplace safety is an important topic because it ensures employee safety, health, and well-being. It generates a lot of discussion among organizational leaders because unsafe work environments can lead to injury or illness. Injury is physical, such as getting hurt while working on a machine. Illness, however, can be physical or mental. Physical illness results from exposure to harmful aspects of the workplace, such as working in an environment where toxic vapors are not properly exhausted. Mental illness results from the stress of working in an unsafe environment, as is the case when employees are so worried about unsafe aspects of their jobs that they are unable to come to work.

Effective designing and implementation of HRM safety strategies minimize injury and illness by eliminating the risk of accidents, stress, and other related problems. These strategies can also increase productivity and profitability while maintaining a healthy and happy workforce.

Safety strategies require an analysis of workplace conditions and are based on the types of jobs being performed. For example, a manufacturing plant has rigorous rules in place when compared to an office due to the protection needed to prevent injury. Along the same lines, employees on a fishing vessel require more safety precautions than employees at a fish market even though there is danger in both workplaces.

Below is an example of an HRM safety strategy implemented at Wilson Paper Supply, a paper towel manufacturing plant located in Chicago, IL. The company employs 250 people including 190 production employees.

Wilson Paper Supply

Please note that this example shows how an HRM strategy can be implemented without using human resource personnel. In this case, the safety team identifies the problem, implements a strategy, and evaluates the success.

Scope

Nick VanDeer is employed as the company's safety manager and oversees all safety-related operations, including a safety team that consists of the plant manager, the quality control manager, and the office manager. The safety team meets once per month to discuss safety concerns in the facility.

Safety problem

The safety team has identified forklift driving in the warehouse as unsafe behavior that needs to be improved. There have not been any documented injuries, but employees have complained to management on three separate occasions that forklift drivers are exhibiting unsafe behavior. It appears that it is only a matter of time before someone gets hurt.

Specific issues with forklift drivers include:

- They sometimes fail to yield for employees walking through the warehouse.

- They sometimes drive forklifts at unsafe speeds.
- They sometimes drive outside the yellow lines that they are instructed to stay within.

Root cause

After interviewing the forklift drivers, the team has determined that the problem is not due to lack of knowledge or misunderstanding. The drivers understand the rules, but they have limited time to get their work done and subsequently do not always follow them.

Potential solutions

The following are potential solutions for correcting the forklift driver's unsafe behavior:

- Terminate the drivers who have exhibited unsafe behavior.
- Threaten to suspend forklift drivers who violate safety rules.
- Meet with the forklift driver's to discuss their unsafe behavior.
- Meet with other managers to discuss the forklift driver's unsafe behavior.
- Meet with all employees to discuss the forklift driver's unsafe behavior.

Chosen solution

The team decides to meet with the forklift drivers to discuss their unsafe behavior. This gives the safety team an opportunity to explain the reasoning behind the rules, and it allows the drivers to ask questions or request clarification. Management and the other employees are not needed in this meeting because the drivers' individual behavior is the specific issue that needs to be addressed.

HRM strategy

Upon meeting with the drivers, Nick VanDeer (safety team leader) starts by explaining to the forklift drivers that some employees have expressed concerns to management about unsafe forklift driving. Nick describes the mentioned drivers' actions below and explains why they are unsafe.

- *The drivers sometimes fail to yield for employees walking through the warehouse*

  Employees often need to cross over forklift paths, so management has designated specific crossing areas. Management realizes the time is important at the paper towel manufacturing plant and drivers want to be efficient at their jobs...but employees should not have to fear accidents when crossing at designated areas.

- *The drivers sometimes drive forklifts at unsafe speeds*

Employees work alongside forklift drivers in some areas of the plant, so management has posted yellow "SLOW" signs in those areas. Again, management realizes that time is important because drivers want to optimize their performance, but employees should not have to worry about being hit by a forklift that is going too fast to stop in time.

- *The drivers sometimes drive outside the yellow lines that they are instructed to stay within*

Employees need to move around to different areas of the plant, so management has drawn yellow lines on the floor to separate forklift paths and employees. Management realizes that it virtually impossible to stay within the yellow lines 100 percent of the time, but employees should not have to fear getting hit by forklifts when they are in their designated areas.

After explaining the safety issues, Nick asks the drivers for suggestions on what could be done to create a safer work environment. One driver suggests that the shipping manager should stop pushing them so hard to get their work done. Nick agrees this is a good idea, but he says that this is not the shipping manager's fault because he is being pressured by the salespeople to fill last-minute orders. However, he can initiate some changes to prevent this from happing on a regular basis. Another driver suggests an incentive program where drivers are rewarded for safe behavior. Nick says safe behavior is expected by all employees, but he can come up with something to help them in this area.

The meeting adjourns, and Nick promises to get back with the drivers the next day with potential resolutions to the problem.

The following day, the safety team again meets with the drivers. Nick proposes the following solutions:

- *Salespeople will be required to put in their order one day before they need to be filled.*

  The sales manager will meet with all salespeople and explain to them that safety is a top priority, and rush orders are creating an unsafe work environment. Understandably, this is not always possible...but it is definitely an area that can and will be improved.

- *Drivers will earn one extra vacation day for every four months that they go without an accident or a complaint.*

  This means the drivers have an opportunity to earn three paid vacation days per year for practicing safe behavior based on written documentation and evaluation by their coworkers.

The drivers agree with Nick's proposal, and the action plan goes into effect at the start of the next work week. Nick expresses confidence in the forklift drivers' ability to be successful, and he tells the drivers that he will share the results with them via an email to their manager at the end of each month.

Evaluation

One year after the safety process has been implemented, the results are analyzed and it is found that strategy is successful. Forklift drivers are practicing safe behavior, and this is verified by the following:

- *Ongoing discussion with plant employees has yielded no complaints since the safety process was implemented.*

- *All drivers have been awarded at least two vacation days since the safety process was implemented.*

- *Tracking of sales data indicates rush orders are down 75 percent since the safety process was implemented.*

Follow-up

For the next two years, the safety team meets every six months to discuss forklift driver safety. They review sales data and employee complaints regarding forklift driver safety. Additionally, they have one forklift driver and two plant employees attend the meeting to voluntary discuss the ongoing success of the safety process. After each meeting, positive feedback is given about the success that is continually being experienced.

Summary

HRM applies strategies designed to meet management objectives, minimize problems, and maximize employee performance. These strategies seek to improve productivity and profitability while adhering to established rules and hiring the best possible workforce. Astute organizational leaders understand that politics, government regulations, and legal concerns have made human resource management more important today than it ever was in the past.

This book is a descriptive and exemplary analysis of human resource management systems used in organizations. It shows how employees and employers interact in real-world situations in order to meet organizational goals. It is educational and informational, and it is written for easy understanding at all reader levels.

Congratulations! You now understand more about human resource management...strategies designed for the management of people and processes in organizations.